Figure

Skating

Journal

This Journal

Belongs To:

_____

ISBN:1977570216
ISBN-13978-1977570215:

Dedication

This journal is dedicated to every girl and boy, man and woman who share a passion for the sport and art of figure skating. May this journal help you in your goals for more centered spins, higher jumps, effortless flow, and a never-ending love of soaring across the ice.

Table of Contents

Welcome to the Figure Skating Journal. This journal will help you to record all your testing accomplishments, competition results, and notes from your lessons. It is meant to help you organize your goals, keep track of your progress, and have a record of your journey in the fantastic sport of figure skating!

In the Goals section, write down the goals that you have for your figure skating progress. Include the date that you made the goal, the date you want to have it completed, and the steps you plan to take to achieve that goal.

In the Testing section, record of all the tests you have attempted. Record the name of the test, date, place, result of the test, and any notes you want to remember about the test.

In the Competition section, record all the competitions you participate in. Include the name of the competition and where it was held, the date, your event name, your result (for example, 1st out of 10), the music that you skated to, and any notes you want to remember about the competition.

In the Lesson Notes section, record notes from your lessons with your coaches. Include the date, rink, the name of the coach, what elements you worked on, and what things you want to remember from the lesson, like tips from your coach or things that worked for an element. Keeping notes on your lessons will be a tremendous help for progressing quickly in your skating journey.

SKATING GOALS

SKATING GOALS

Skating Goal	Date Made	Goal Date	Steps to Achieve Goal	Done

SKATING GOALS

Skating Goal	Date Made	Goal Date	Steps to Achieve Goal	Done

SKATING GOALS

Skating Goal	Date Made	Goal Date	Steps to Achieve Goal	Done

SKATING GOALS

Skating Goal	Date Made	Goal Date	Steps to Achieve Goal	Done

TESTING RECORDS

TESTING RECORDS

Test Name	Date	Place	Result	Notes

TESTING RECORDS

Test Name	Date	Place	Result	Notes

TESTING RECORDS

Test Name	Date	Place	Result	Notes

TESTING RECORDS

Test Name	Date	Place	Result	Notes

COMPETITIONS

COMPETITIONS

Competition Name	Date	Event	Result	Music	Notes

Competition Name	Date	Event	Result	Music	Notes

COMPETITIONS

Competition Name	Date	Event	Result	Music	Notes

Competition Name	Date	Event	Result	Music	Notes

COMPETITIONS

Competition Name	Date	Event	Result	Music	Notes

COMPETITIONS

Competition Name	Date	Event	Result	Music	Notes

LESSON NOTES

LESSON NOTES

Lesson Date	Place	Coach
Elements Practiced	**Things to Remember**	

Lesson Date	Place	Coach
Elements Practiced	**Things to Remember**	

LESSON NOTES

Lesson Date	Place	Coach
Elements Practiced	Things to Remember	

Lesson Date	Place	Coach
Elements Practiced	Things to Remember	

Lesson Notes

Lesson Date	Place	Coach

Elements Practiced	Things to Remember

Lesson Date	Place	Coach

Elements Practiced	Things to Remember

Lesson Notes

Lesson Date	Place	Coach
Elements Practiced	Things to Remember	

Lesson Date	Place	Coach
Elements Practiced	Things to Remember	

LESSON NOTES

Lesson Date	Place	Coach

Elements Practiced	Things to Remember

Lesson Date	Place	Coach

Elements Practiced	Things to Remember

LESSON NOTES

Lesson Date	Place	Coach
Elements Practiced	Things to Remember	

Lesson Date	Place	Coach
Elements Practiced	Things to Remember	

LESSON NOTES

Lesson Date	Place	Coach
Elements Practiced	Things to Remember	

Lesson Date	Place	Coach
Elements Practiced	Things to Remember	

LESSON NOTES

Lesson Date	Place	Coach

Elements Practiced	Things to Remember

Lesson Date	Place	Coach

Elements Practiced	Things to Remember

LESSON NOTES

Lesson Date	Place	Coach

Elements Practiced	Things to Remember

Lesson Date	Place	Coach

Elements Practiced	Things to Remember

LESSON NOTES

Lesson Date	Place	Coach

Elements Practiced	Things to Remember

Lesson Date	Place	Coach

Elements Practiced	Things to Remember

LESSON NOTES

Lesson Date	Place	Coach
Elements Practiced	Things to Remember	

Lesson Date	Place	Coach
Elements Practiced	Things to Remember	

LESSON NOTES

Lesson Date	Place	Coach

Elements Practiced	Things to Remember

Lesson Date	Place	Coach

Elements Practiced	Things to Remember

LESSON NOTES

Lesson Date	Place	Coach
Elements Practiced	Things to Remember	

Lesson Date	Place	Coach
Elements Practiced	Things to Remember	

Lesson Date	Place	Coach
Elements Practiced	Things to Remember	

Lesson Date	Place	Coach
Elements Practiced	Things to Remember	

LESSON NOTES

Lesson Date	Place	Coach
Elements Practiced	Things to Remember	

Lesson Date	Place	Coach
Elements Practiced	Things to Remember	

LESSON NOTES

Lesson Date	Place	Coach
Elements Practiced	Things to Remember	

Lesson Date	Place	Coach
Elements Practiced	Things to Remember	

LESSON NOTES

Lesson Date	Place	Coach
Elements Practiced	Things to Remember	

Lesson Date	Place	Coach
Elements Practiced	Things to Remember	

LESSON NOTES

Lesson Date	Place	Coach

Elements Practiced	Things to Remember

Lesson Date	Place	Coach

Elements Practiced	Things to Remember

LESSON NOTES

Lesson Date	Place	Coach
Elements Practiced	Things to Remember	

Lesson Date	Place	Coach
Elements Practiced	Things to Remember	

LESSON NOTES

Lesson Date	Place	Coach

Elements Practiced	Things to Remember

Lesson Date	Place	Coach

Elements Practiced	Things to Remember

LESSON NOTES

Lesson Date	Place	Coach
Elements Practiced	Things to Remember	

Lesson Date	Place	Coach
Elements Practiced	Things to Remember	

Lesson Date	Place	Coach
Elements Practiced	Things to Remember	

Lesson Date	Place	Coach
Elements Practiced	Things to Remember	

LESSON NOTES

Lesson Date	Place	Coach
Elements Practiced	Things to Remember	

Lesson Date	Place	Coach
Elements Practiced	Things to Remember	

LESSON NOTES

Lesson Date	Place	Coach
Elements Practiced	Things to Remember	

Lesson Date	Place	Coach
Elements Practiced	Things to Remember	

Lesson Date	Place	Coach
Elements Practiced	Things to Remember	

Lesson Date	Place	Coach
Elements Practiced	Things to Remember	

LESSON NOTES

Lesson Date	Place	Coach
Elements Practiced	Things to Remember	

Lesson Date	Place	Coach
Elements Practiced	Things to Remember	

LESSON NOTES

Lesson Date	Place	Coach
Elements Practiced	Things to Remember	

Lesson Date	Place	Coach
Elements Practiced	Things to Remember	

LESSON NOTES

Lesson Date	Place	Coach

Elements Practiced	Things to Remember

Lesson Date	Place	Coach

Elements Practiced	Things to Remember

Lesson Date	Place	Coach
Elements Practiced	Things to Remember	

Lesson Date	Place	Coach
Elements Practiced	Things to Remember	

LESSON NOTES

Lesson Date	Place	Coach
Elements Practiced	Things to Remember	

Lesson Date	Place	Coach
Elements Practiced	Things to Remember	

Lesson Date	Place	Coach
Elements Practiced	Things to Remember	

Lesson Date	Place	Coach
Elements Practiced	Things to Remember	

Lesson Date	Place	Coach
Elements Practiced	Things to Remember	

Lesson Date	Place	Coach
Elements Practiced	Things to Remember	

LESSON NOTES

Lesson Date	Place	Coach
Elements Practiced	Things to Remember	

Lesson Date	Place	Coach
Elements Practiced	Things to Remember	

LESSON NOTES

Lesson Date	Place	Coach
Elements Practiced	Things to Remember	

Lesson Date	Place	Coach
Elements Practiced	Things to Remember	

Lesson Date	Place	Coach
Elements Practiced	Things to Remember	

Lesson Date	Place	Coach
Elements Practiced	Things to Remember	

LESSON NOTES

Lesson Date	Place	Coach
Elements Practiced	Things to Remember	

Lesson Date	Place	Coach
Elements Practiced	Things to Remember	

LESSON NOTES

Lesson Date	Place	Coach
Elements Practiced	Things to Remember	

Lesson Date	Place	Coach
Elements Practiced	Things to Remember	

LESSON NOTES

Lesson Date	Place	Coach
Elements Practiced	Things to Remember	

Lesson Date	Place	Coach
Elements Practiced	Things to Remember	

LESSON NOTES

Lesson Date	Place	Coach
Elements Practiced	**Things to Remember**	

Lesson Date	Place	Coach
Elements Practiced	**Things to Remember**	

LESSON NOTES

Lesson Date	Place	Coach
Elements Practiced	Things to Remember	

Lesson Date	Place	Coach
Elements Practiced	Things to Remember	

Lesson Date	Place	Coach
Elements Practiced	Things to Remember	

Lesson Date	Place	Coach
Elements Practiced	Things to Remember	

LESSON NOTES

Lesson Date	Place	Coach
Elements Practiced	Things to Remember	

Lesson Date	Place	Coach
Elements Practiced	Things to Remember	

LESSON NOTES

Lesson Date	Place	Coach
Elements Practiced	Things to Remember	

Lesson Date	Place	Coach
Elements Practiced	Things to Remember	

LESSON NOTES

Lesson Date	Place	Coach
Elements Practiced	Things to Remember	

Lesson Date	Place	Coach
Elements Practiced	Things to Remember	

Lesson Date	Place	Coach
Elements Practiced	Things to Remember	

Lesson Date	Place	Coach
Elements Practiced	Things to Remember	

LESSON NOTES

Lesson Date	Place	Coach
Elements Practiced	Things to Remember	

Lesson Date	Place	Coach
Elements Practiced	Things to Remember	

LESSON NOTES

Lesson Date	Place	Coach
Elements Practiced	Things to Remember	

Lesson Date	Place	Coach
Elements Practiced	Things to Remember	

LESSON NOTES

Lesson Date	Place	Coach
Elements Practiced	Things to Remember	

Lesson Date	Place	Coach
Elements Practiced	Things to Remember	

LESSON NOTES

Lesson Date	Place	Coach
Elements Practiced	Things to Remember	

Lesson Date	Place	Coach
Elements Practiced	Things to Remember	

LESSON NOTES

Lesson Date	Place	Coach
Elements Practiced	Things to Remember	

Lesson Date	Place	Coach
Elements Practiced	Things to Remember	